WHAT'S UP, DOC?

WHAT'S UP, DOC?

Compiled and Edited by
REVILO SNIVIB

UNABRIDGED

PAN BOOKS LTD : LONDON

First published in Great Britain 1962
by Frederick Muller Ltd.
This edition published 1965 by Pan Books Ltd.,
33 Tothill Street, London, S.W.1

ISBN 0 330 02727 1

2nd Printing 1971

© Charm Books Inc., New York, 1961

*Printed in Great Britain by Richard Clay (The Chaucer Press), Ltd.,
Bungay, Suffolk*

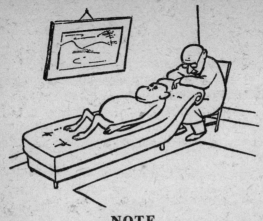

NOTE

'The man who laughs is a doctor without a diploma,' and with this thought in mind your editor began a safari into the antiseptic world of doctors and nurses to see if any funny bones were left over on the floor of the operating room and if ticklish ribs were plentiful among the men (and women) in white.

Consultations with the wheel-chair and bedpan set proved that even patients could see the funny side of illness. With the help of cartoonists and story tellers, your investigator covered the medical scene from diagnosis to prognosis, gathering material from doctors, psychiatrists, nurses, orderlies and ambulance drivers.

The result is this home dispensary of clinical quips, medical merriment and humorous bedside mannerisms which we hope will be a relaxing tonic for one and all.

As someone once said,

'HE WHO LAUGHS, LASTS!'

DOCTOR'S GAM-BIT

Even though he was a practising doctor, old Doc Horner was a hypochondriac and lived in constant fear of the paralytic stroke he was sure would carry him off some day.

One evening the crusty old bachelor MD was entertaining a pretty young nurse in his apartment where they were playing chess. Doc Horner suddenly fell back in his chair with a frightened look.

'My time has come!' he moaned. 'I've had a stroke and my whole right side is paralysed!'

'How can you be so sure?' asked the little nurse as she tried to calm him down.

'I've been feeling and pinching and tickling my leg for the last hour and there's no sensation there!'

'Cheer up, Doc!' said the little nurse with a grin, 'that was MY leg you were working over!'

There was the pregnant nurse whose theme song was 'Witch Doctor'.

PASS WORD

'Knock knock!'
'Who's there, friend . . . or enema?'

'Nurse! . . . *what* was he doing yesterday?'

IDIOTIC INDEX OF MEDICAL MERRIMENT

DRYDOCK: Medico athirst

HORMONE: Underpaid floozie

SCAR: The best Havana

DOCTOR'S BAG: That ugly nurse he hired last week

BAND AID: Musician's favourite soft drink

BACTERIA: Rear exit of the Cafeteria

COLIC: The way the student combs his hair

OXYGEN TENT: A large size in inflatable bras

QUACK: Crooked duck with a medical degree

ABDOMEN: Bowl-shaped cavity containing the organs of indigestion

CLAVICLE: Ancient musical instrument

STERNUM: Roman canned heat

PARTURITION: Daddy pays the school fee

MICROSCOPE SLIDE: Flea ski

PHARMACOPOEIA: The druggist had to 'go'

CLINIC: What Mrs Mefooskey does in her house every spring

BRONCHOSCOPE: Eyeglasses to watch old horses with

HOMEOPATH: The road back to mother

NURSE: A pan-handler

CARDIOLOGY: The art of drawing to an inside straight

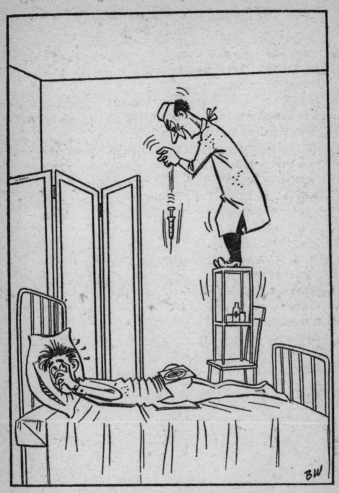

'I find it easier that way, since I was in Bomber
Command during the war!'

'Today, we study female anatomy!'

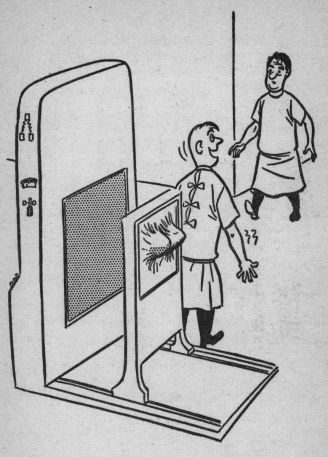

'Boy! I just X-rayed that new film-star from Rome!'

PRE-MEDICAL OPINION

'Thermometers,' says old Doctor Frazzle as he looks over the current crop of medical students, 'aren't the only things that are graduated and get degrees without having any brains.'

METHOD IN HER BADNESS

MILLIE: 'I've got a terrible headache!'

DILLIE: 'When I have a headache my husband soothes all the pain away; all he has to do is to rub the back of my neck then caress my forehead lightly then plant a little kiss on my mouth and before you know it: no more headache! Why don't you try it?'

MILLIE: 'Think I will. When's your husband get home?'

RESTRAINED TO BE SEEN

An eye doctor I know is highly in favour of mixed sunbathing in the raw as a healthful occupation. When asked why, he smiles and answers: 'Did you ever see a blind nudist?'

SLAM! BANG! THANK YOU . . . MAN!

Sanford Isotope, junior statistician, had a nervous breakdown last week. He was trying to take an inventory at a rabbit farm.

'How do you flush this thing anyway?'

QUICK REVISION

The sailor walked into the tattoo parlour and asked for a quick estimate on a special job. Some years before he had had a full length picture of his girl friend tattooed on his manly frame and he wanted some changes made. The artist asked to see the design and the sailor took off his shirt. The tattoo expert gave a gasp of surprise, and admiration: here was the most beautiful work of skin art he had ever seen, a beautiful nude girl done with almost perfect realism.

'Why,' asked the artist, 'do you want to change such a masterpiece?'

The sailor snapped back, 'Ever since I had that appendicitis operation, she's too d— *realistic*!'

OUT OF BOUNDS

SHOPKEEPER: 'Hey, you, no smoking in here!'

BONE HEAD: 'Whaddya mean, I just bought this cigar right here in this shop!'

SHOPKEEPER: 'So I sell you a laxative, that gives you the right to use it here?'

'Have you an appointment?'

'Speak softly so I can take down notes!'

'It's nothing serious – come back for a check-up
in nine months!'

BELOW ZERO

GOOSEPIMPLE: 'Doc, I couldn't sleep a wink last night, I was so cold. Freezing!'

DOC: 'Did your teeth chatter?'

GOOSEPIMPLE: 'How should I know? We never sleep together!'

THE AGE OF URANIUM

Two Irish charwomen were discussing the H-Bomb.

'Oh!' said Mrs Muldoon, 'what a terrible thing it is now, that Haych-Bomb! Why it's liable to blow you all the way from here to maternity!'

'Begorrah!' answered Mrs O'Toole, 'and ye'd niver know who to blame!'

QUICK, A TRANSFUSION!

The drunk staggered into the accident ward and stood weaving in the glare of the hospital light. The neck of a pint of cheap red wine protruded from his hip pocket. The student nurse cried out:

'Oh, that man's badly injured on the buttocks!'

The bum quickly put his hand to his seat and then brought it up to his face. Staring at the red stains he muttered:

'That BETTER be blood!'

'Report on the patient in 68:
Final hormone injection given!'

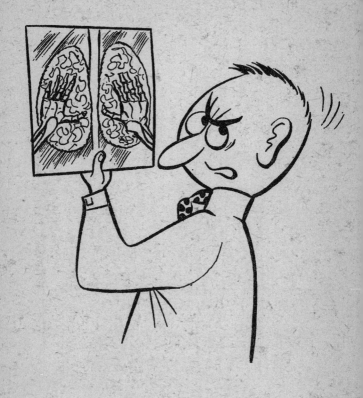

'Gertrude! . . . I want to know the doctor's name
who took your chest X-ray!'

'. . . . And one suppository before his bedtime!'

REVEILLE WITH BEVERLEY

DOCTOR: 'My examination shows you have poor
reflexes. Do you ever wake up with a
jerk?'

BEVERLEY: 'Why, Doc! I'm pretty choosey about my
boy friends!'

DEPARTMENT OF UTTER TRANSFUSION

The old lady had just returned from two weeks at
a Continental holiday resort.

'Where did you stay, Mama?' her doctor son
asked.

'At the Montagne Plasma.'

'Mama!' the doctor exclaimed, 'plasma is blood,
You mean the Montagne PLAZA!'

'Listen, my son,' the old lady replied. 'Ten pounds
a day for a room without meals . . . that is *blood*!'

STORM SIGNALS

ANXIOUS: 'Doc, these spots! I'm all covered with
rashes and spots!'

DOC: 'Mister, I hate to have to tell you this, but
you have a venereal disease.'

ANXIOUS: 'Oh thank heavens, Doc! And here I
thought all the time that it was measles!'

'It's a boy!'

ACCIDENT AWARD

The pert little girl jumped into the cab and told the driver:

'Quick, get me to the fraternity ward!'

'Look, Lady,' the driver answered, 'you mean the *maternity* ward.'

'I guess so,' she answered, 'but hurry, I've got to see an outern!'

'Outern!' the driver shouted, 'you mean *intern!*'

'Oh!' the girl answered, 'fraternity-maternity . . . intern-outern, just get me there quick. . . . I think I'm stagnant!'

A DRUG ON THE CARPET

The old resident doctor was advising the third-year student on the use of miracle sulpha drugs.

'There are several varieties of sulpha drugs,' he explained. 'For example there is sulpha-*diozone* which is prescribed for pneumonia; boils respond to treatment with sulpha-*thiozol* . . . and come to think of it, since a newly married man like you wants to hold off from having any kids in the near future, for *your* case I'd prescribe sulpha-*denial!*'

'BARK!'

'Thank you, Doctor – I can always depend on you for business!'

NO DANGER THERE

Bumpsa Daisey, the striptease queen, was a tremendous hypochondriac and at the least symptom would run to see the doctor.

One morning she appeared at a doctor's office and described all kinds of horrible symptoms to the patiently listening physician.

'Doctor,' she wound up, 'I'm real sick! Will I die?' The doctor smiled.

'See here,' he said, 'it's all your imagination. Nothing could kill *you*! . . . now just to be sure, take off your clothes. . . .'

Bumpsa Daisey reached for a shoulder strap then looked at the elderly physician for a moment then said:

'Doc . . . it might kill you!'

ALL CLEAR?

There is the guy in show business who, when he is told by his doctor to gargle, always takes an enema instead: the guy's a ventriloquist.

'The doctor wants you to drink it at room
temperature so keep it there a while longer.'

'Can't tell if you've got asthma or a rusty joint!'

COMPLICATIONS

MANY A SLIP TWIXT THE HICCUP
AND LIP

The asylum inmate was being treated in the fever therapy room and was locked into a device called a 'hot box' which held him motionless. Doctor's orders were that the patient's temperature be taken every five minutes and a record made on his chart.

The young nurse gave the inmate a rectal thermometer then left the room for a moment. When she came back she was astonished to find the thermometer in the patient's mouth.

'How did the thermometer get THERE?' she asked. 'You are strapped in and cannot possibly move!'

The inmate smiled.

'I hiccuped!' he said slyly.

33

'Stick to dairy products, vegetables, fruit, but at all costs avoid MEAT!'

'Ready, aim, . . . fire!'

A GLAND AND GLORIOUS FEELING

Dr Moto, Oriental monkey-gland specialist, relates the following experiment during the war when there developed a shortage of monkeys. In desperation he substituted small onions for the usual glands. The plan worked out and Dr Moto was pleased to lecture on the results before the Academy of Medicine.

'Onion,' he stated, 'work very well as substitute with only one objection: when man get very great urge he get *tears* in his eyes!'

LOVE, HONOUR AND OH, BABY!

Mandy, the coloured woman, went to the doctor with her troubles. It seems that after six years of married life she still had not had a baby. The doctor made a careful examination and explained to her carefully the reason why she was unable to have a child.

'Mandy,' he said, 'you have an insufficient passage and if you ever have a baby it'll be a miracle.'

Sad at heart Mandy went home and told her husband the unhappy news.

'Rastus,' she said, 'the doctor say there's a fish in the passage an' if I ever has a baby it'll be a mackerel!'

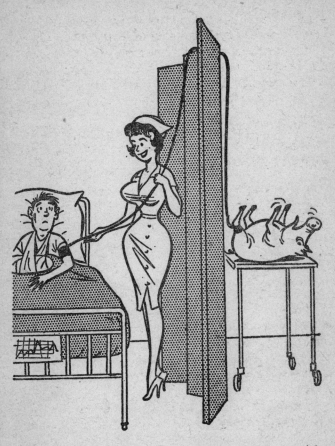

'Sorry, we can't disclose the identity of a donor with *your* type blood.'

'The Doctors are Operating!'

FRIENDS, ROMANS AND PSYCHIATRIST LEND ME YOUR EARS!

YOUNG PSYCHIATRIST: 'Tell me, Doctor, how on earth can you stand to listen to your patients on the couch, day after day as they pour out all that misery and frustration, all that mess of troubles?'

OLD PSYCHIATRIST: 'Who listens?'

LAST WORD

ATTORNEY AT LAW: 'Say, Doctor, I'm always being pumped for free advice when I go to parties. Do you get the same thing too?'

DOCTOR OF MEDICINE: 'Yes, Charlie, I do, but I usually break in right in the middle of a chapter of symptoms and say out loud: "Strip off your clothes." Then I'm left alone for the rest of the evening.'

'No baby! – that's *papa*, not mama!'

'Check him over at your end, then call me back!'

'You lost a lot of weight since your appendix
operation!'

PRIVATE WARD

'Tell me, Tom,' asked the visitor in the luxurious private hospital room, 'since you can afford all this plus the services of a full-time private nurse, why did you pick such an ugly old bat to look after you?'

'Well,' Tom answered, 'when she begins to look good to me I know I'm getting well!'

GOODBYE AND BED RIDDANCE

GUY: 'Doctor, you won't believe it but I'm troubled with a bad case of housemaid's knee! I don't know what to do – it keeps me awake all night!'

DOC: 'Why don't you try sleeping alone?'

PSYCHO-ANALYSE YOURSELF

Just pull up a couch and lie back. Relax and see how good you are at self-analysis by answering the following questions with the first word that occurs to you.

1. What does a cow have four of and a woman two?
2. What does a dog do in the yard that you have to step over?
3. What is the first thing newlyweds do after they are alone?
4. What is generally found in bird cages and some people are full of it.

Answers on page 46.

'Three days I'm eating 'em and *now* you tell me!'

Answers to self-analysis quiz on page 44.

1. FEET
2. HOLE
3. TALK
4. GRIT

COLOUR BLIND

The little man was worried.

'Doctor,' he said, 'I've got a problem. My wife is a natural blonde; all her family are blondes. I am dark haired, and that has run in my family for years. All our kids are either blonde or dark haired and now all of a sudden . . . my wife has a redheaded baby! Now I'm a lighthouse keeper and believe me that lighthouse is so far out we never have any visitors! So how do you explain it?'

The doctor examined the patient and found him sound and well.

'Tell me,' the doctor asked, 'how often do you have relations with your wife? . . . twice a week?'

The little man shook his head.

'Once a month?' the doctor asked.

The little man shook his head.

'Once every six months?' the doctor demanded.

'Oh, no!' the little man answered.

'Once a year then?' the doctor asked in an exasperated tone.

'Well . . .' said the little man hesitantly, '. . . maybe.'

'That explains it!' said the doctor triumphantly. 'You're just a little *rusty*, that's all!'

46

'Yeah! . . . but supposin' all of a sudden I gotta GO?'

SODA JERK

Belinda, a pretty young thing, came to ask Doc Capsule if he was able to disguise castor oil so that it wouldn't taste so bad.

'Why certainly,' the doctor said. 'I am just going to make a chocolate ice-cream soda for my daughter. Would you like one too?'

'Yes, please,' said Belinda as the doctor began mixing the drinks.

After she had finished the soda she asked Doc Capsule:

'Now, let's get back to the subject of disguising castor oil. How do you do it?'

'Ah ha!' cried Doc Capsule, with a merry twinkle in his eye, 'there was a double dose of castor oil in that soda you just had!'

'Oh NO!' wailed Belinda, 'and I wanted the castor oil for my *sister*!'

MARATHON

DOCTOR: 'How's the patient in 402?'
NURSE: 'Gasping for breath!'
DOCTOR: 'What's the matter with him?'
NURSE: 'He's been chasing me around the room.'

STRIKE ACTION

There was a dumb nurse who stayed home from the hospital because she thought it was being picketed. A friend had called her to say they had labour trouble in the maternity ward.

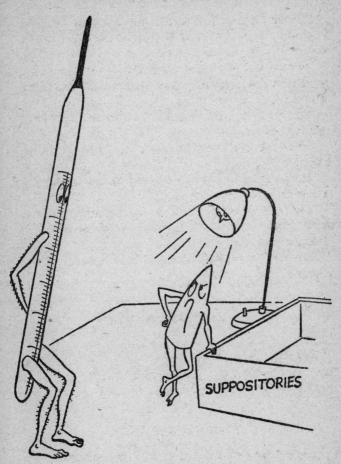

'At least we have one thing in common!'

FORCED INTO HABIT

Elmer Slurp injured his right leg and needed a doctor right away. But there was no physician within fifty miles. Time was running out and he soon might lose his leg. A local veterinary surgeon learned of his plight and agreed to see what he could do to save Elmer's leg. Soon the patient was placed on the operating table in the animal hospital and the vet went to work. During the operation he found that his patient needed a muscle graft. The only ligament available was a dog's thigh muscle left over from an operation performed that morning. The doctor thought he'd take a chance—and sure enough the emergency muscle-graft worked. Two weeks later Elmer walked about on his own feet like a new man.

But since then he can never pass a fire hydrant.

LADY IN WAITING

NOSEY: 'Tell me, Dearie, are you going to have a baby?'

POSEY: 'No, I'm just carrying this one for a friend.'

'Come again!'

'Next!'

ALL IN A NAME

BABY SPECIALIST: 'Miss Freeble, do you know what we doctors call a man who does not believe in birth control?'

NURSE: 'Why no, Doctor.'

BABY SPECIALIST: 'Daddy!'

COSTUME PARTY

The hospital staff was planning a costume party and the young nurses were discussing the outfits to be worn.

'What do you think old Sourpuss, the matron, is going to wear?' one pretty young thing asked.

'With her varicose veins,' her friend answered, 'she could go as a road map!'

HOLD EVERYTHING!

DOCTOR: 'Do any of you student nurses know the difference between amnesia and magnesia?'

STUDENTS: ? ? ? ? ?

DOCTOR: 'Girls, the patient who has amnesia doesn't know where he's going.'

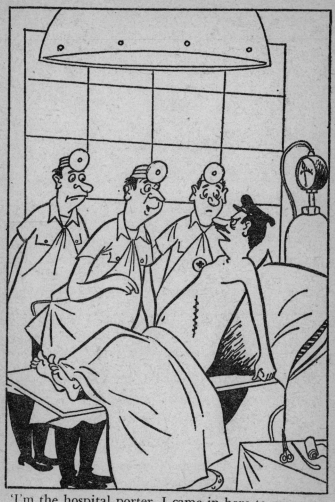

'I'm the hospital porter, I came in here to mop up
and the first thing I knew . . . !'

'If that's the way it's going to be, at least be a gentle-
man and take off your gloves!'

THERE'S SOMETHING ABOUT
A SOLDIER . . .

Flick and Smacker wanted to escape military service so they went and had all their teeth pulled out. When they reported at the reception centre they were shoved into line for the medical examination. Somehow in the shuffle Flick got separated from Smacker by a huge grimy coal heaver.

When the moving line of bare-skinned recruits reached Smacker the medico asked him if he wanted to claim an exemption from service.

'Yeah, Doc,' mumbled Smacker, 'I lost all my teeth!' The doctor shoved his hand into Smacker's mouth and felt around his gums.

'Not a tooth in him!' he exclaimed. 'This man is deferred! Next man!'

The grimy coal heaver stepped up.

'What's your claim to exemption?' the doctor demanded.

'Doc,' the man answered, 'I got the worst case of haemorrhoids you ever heard of!'

The doctor made the usual examination with his fingers and the coal heaver yelled with pain.

'No doubt about it!' the doctor exclaimed. 'It's the worst case on record . . . next man!'

Flick hesitated. The doctor beckoned him with his examining finger.

'Come on, man, what's your claim for exemption?'

Flick gulped, looked at the beckoning finger, then dashed wildly past the doctor shouting:

'Just gimme a gun, Doc, I'm a fightin' fool!'

'Don't be afraid, you're only under observation here!'

'I highly recommend a few nights off with the
boys . . .'

'Hear you've got a sick elephant!'

FLY IN AND OUT OF THE OINTMENT

An anxious woman brought her husband to the doctor's office. She explained that he had lately taken to going around with his fingers thrust up his nostrils and wouldn't remove them, no matter how much she asked him to. The doctor, using psychology, asked the man why he persisted in such an awkward habit.

'Because there's a fly up there, Doc!' the man answered.

The doctor decided to humour his patient. Calling his nurse aside he gave her whispered instructions to catch a fly in a specimen bottle and hand it to him without the patient seeing it. When this was done the doctor pretended to examine the patient and after a moment suddenly produced the fly in the bottle, saying, 'There! We've got him out!'

The patient was delighted and his wife took him home. An hour later the phone rang in the doctor's office. It was the anxious wife.

'Doctor!' she said frantically, 'he's got his fingers back there again!'

'But,' the doctor answered, 'I thought we had him convinced that it was out.'

'I know,' the woman wailed, 'but now he's trying to keep it from getting back in!'

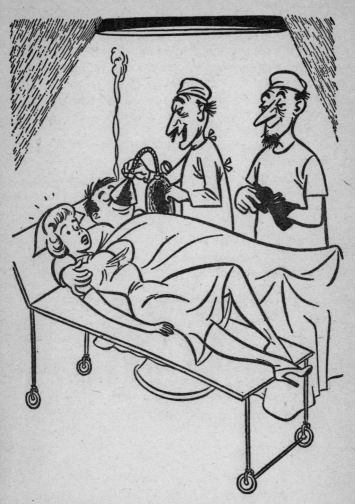

'You have to cater to some patients!'

'Next time *warn* me before you take that medicine!'

'You're fine, Doctor! How am I?'

A PULSE THAT RATES

The voluptuous young nurse came into the doctor's inner office for the third time.

'Doctor,' she said, 'I'm having trouble with that patient you told me to examine. I've taken his pulse three times now and it's beating at an incredible rate. What'll I do?'

The doctor looked at her for a moment, and said, 'How old is the patient, Miss Jones?'

'Twenty-one.'

'Well, try once more, but this time button your blouse.'

HOPE SPRINGS INFERNALLY

Sedgewick Hassenfeffer received a telegram informing him that his mother-in-law was gravely ill at the memorial hospital. He went to the phone, called up the chief surgeon and asked if there was any hope for the old lady.

'That, my friend,' the doctor answered, 'all depends on which way you're hoping!'

'He's from the old-fashioned Country-Doctor School!'

'After you!'

'The wife and kids!'

LAST WORD

Here lie the bones of Gertie Peltzer
Who burst while drinking Halka Zeltzer;
Although she's attained a heavenly rest
She should have waited till it effervesced!

WIND AND FRESH HEIR

The young widow came to the doctor's surgery to find out if she really was about to have a baby. The doctor examined her and then assured her that she had nothing to worry about – she only had a simple gas condition.

Three months later, with a considerably enlarged waistline, the widow returned and asked if by now it was not obvious that she was soon to be a mother. The MD gave her a thorough exam then pronounced his verdict: gas in the stomach.

'Just let it pass,' he said, 'let it pass and you'll be all right.'

Some few years later while walking down the street the doctor was surprised to see the young widow with a little boy, dressed in a sailor suit.

'Ah, you're married again, I see,' said the doctor.

'Like fun!' the widow snapped back. 'See this?' She pointed to the little boy. 'I followed your advice and let it pass, put the *gas* in a sailor suit and called him George!'

'You may undress now . . . !'

'I'm so absent-minded I was going to write the prescription with the thermometer. . . . Say! Where IS my fountain pen?'

'Fine time to tell me you got to go!'

JUST WHAT THE DOCTOR HOARDED

Speedy Gonzales, lightning Latin, met a beautiful 'Doll' at a cocktail party and over the martinis managed to promote himself up to her boudoir. A noise of keys rattling in the door interrupted the festivities and Speedy Gonzales, quick as a flash, was fully dressed and adopting a 'bedside manner' with the 'Doll'.

'. . . take a pill every four hours,' he said as the husband came storming into the room, 'and stay out of draughts.'

'Talk fast, Gonzales,' whispered the wife, 'my husband is a *real* doctor!'

AIN'T WHAT SHE USED TO BE

'Doctor,' the forty-year-old woman said, 'I'm losing my "sting"! After the first one I'm still rarin' to go and ready for anything . . . the second leaves me a bit on the weak side but the third is almost too much. . . . I can't take it!'

'Madam,' said the doctor, 'since the first one seems to agree with you so well and there's no ill effect, I would try to be more moderate and limit myself to just one. If you feel a second is absolutely necessary, rest for a couple of hours in between, but cut out the third altogether!'

'But, Doctor,' she protested, 'I can't cut it out! I live on the third floor of that block of flats and there's no lift!'

'They never told me it'd be like this in medical school!'

'I'm worried about my English bride, Doctor. She spent a restless night!'

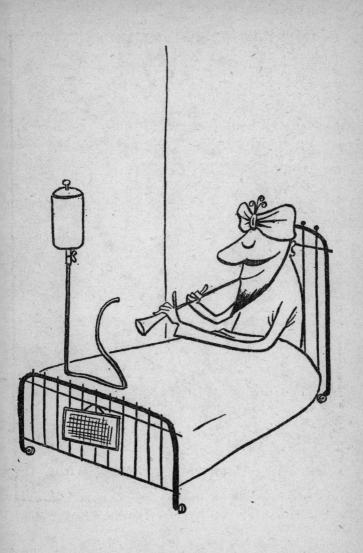

POP GO THE MEASLES!

Weepy Willie was afraid of catching the very diseases he was attempting, as a novice doctor, to cure. Every time he was told to go and treat a patient with an infectious disease he would find some excuse not to show up and some other doctor had to do his work. One morning the chief physician ordered him to attend a bad case of measles in the children's ward. Weepy Willie began to make excuses, trying to get out of the case.

'Now, Doctor,' he protested, 'I can't expose myself to any contagious disease!'

'Well, in that case,' said the head doctor in disgust, 'why don't you specialize? . . . You sure can't catch haemorrhoids!'

LEFT! RIGHT!

INSURANCE DOCTOR: 'Mr Bealzey, that pain in your leg is simply due to old age.'

MR BEALZEY: 'Old age like heck! My other leg is just the same age and it feels fine!'

FORMULA NUMBER EIGHT AND A HALF

There is a brand-new hair restorer on the market. It won't grow hair, it just shrinks your head so that what hair you had left around the edges will be enough to cover up the shiny part.

'. . . And you should all become acquainted with the
better cuts!'

WHAT THIS COUNTRY NEEDS . . .

DR: 'What YOU need, young man, is some sun and air.'

MR: 'Yes, Doctor, but my wife doesn't want any kids!'

GETTING DOWN TO BUSINESS

Dr Lucius K. Bladder and his wife were visiting a museum. A flashy blonde in a tight-fitting black satin dress rustled by and trilled a musical hello to the doctor, and waved a dainty hand.

'And who, may I ask, is THAT?' the doctor's wife demanded in a grim voice.

'Oh,' the doctor answered with a shrug, 'just someone I met on a professional basis.'

'Which basis . . . yours . . . or hers?'

THE MASTER BUILDER

The junior architect asked the head of the building firm for three days off, right in the middle of a rush job.

'My wife is about to have a baby,' he explained to his boss.

'See here, young man,' the senior architect answered, 'you're only needed to lay the foundations. The formal opening can come off without you!'

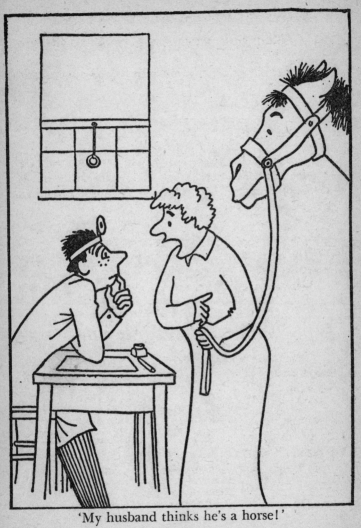

'My husband thinks he's a horse!'

'See that ye include the cat, Doctor!'

'I'll be ready in a moment!'

'Convinced?'

'What are my plans? I'm taking the next boat to
Australia!'

'Eeney . . . meeney . . . miney . . . mo! . . . it's your
turn!'

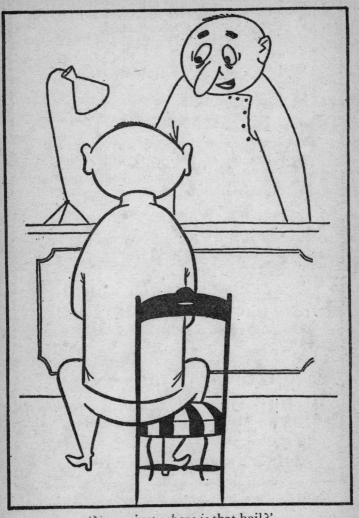

'Now – just *where is* that boil?'

LOOK BEFORE YOU LEAP

Frederika Schmaltz, who lives on the fourth floor of our block of flats, has St Vitus dance. Last week she married a riveter and now the whole place is jumping!

PINK SLIP

'Doctor Jones, as staff psychiatrist you are setting a very bad example! This is the fifth complaint I have had about your molesting female patients and student nurses. Have you anything to say for yourself?'

'No, sir.'

'Very well, Jones . . . turn in your couch: you're fired!'

KEEP MUM ABOUT THIS!

There was the millionairess who went on a champagne diet. In less than six weeks she took off £1,500!

SOMETHING TO GUSH ABOUT

The fact that I'm a millionaire today is due to a lucky stroke. My uncle in Texas had one!

IN THE FINAL ANALYSIS

Psychiatry is simply when you lie down and talk things over. Some people have a different name for it.

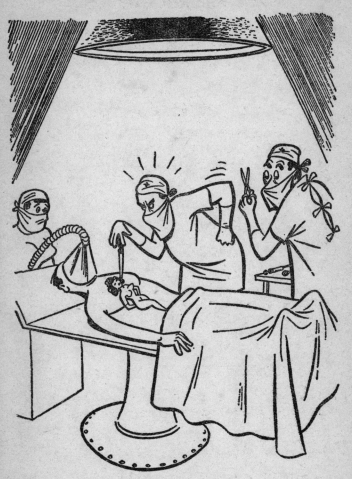

'Doctor, that's your wife!'

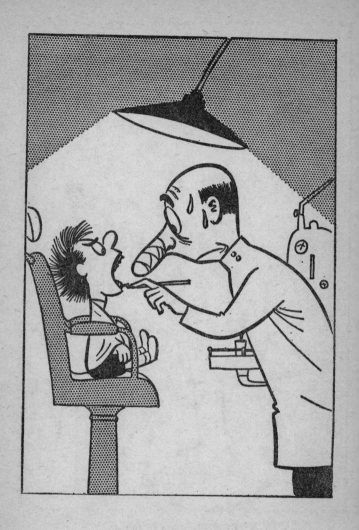

'That's not your son, it's the doctor who just
FAINTED!'

THE RIGHT PRESCRIPTION

'Funniest case in my forty years of medical practice came up when I was called in to treat a side show freak,' Dr Forceps related one evening at the County Medical Society.

'I was called down to the fairground by the circus management to treat the half-man-half-woman. I found the patient to be in a very run down condition. So I prescribed a hormone injection and a dose of Lydia Tinkham's vegetable compound and after that he was a new woman!'

WHAT THE TRAFFIC WILL BARE

Dr Morris Q. Mental, famous psychiatrist, was advising a young doctor.

'Young man,' he said, 'you must always remember this about the practice of psychiatry: in a ten-guinea-a-day private room the patients are called *neurotics*, but in the free clinic downstairs they're just plain *nuts*!'

SICK LEAVE

SHOP FOREMAN : 'What's this about "lazy" Jake being out sick and not able to work for a whole month? I think he's just faking, Doctor!'

COMPANY DOCTOR : 'You're right . . . but compensation has set in!'

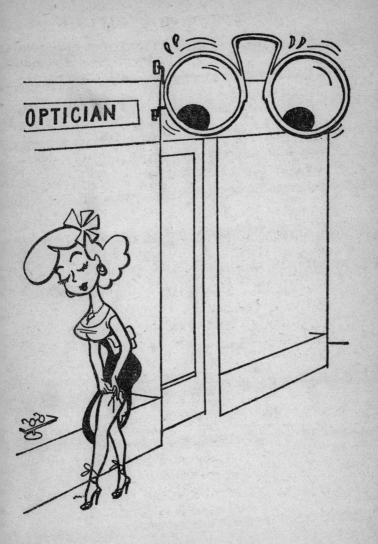

OPTICIAN

QUACK QUACK

DR BLACK: 'Hey, what's the idea of calling in another doctor after I've been treating you for six months!'

MAURY BUND: 'That other doctor said your diagnosis is all wrong, so what do you have to say to that?'

DR BLUE: 'Just wait . . . the autopsy never lies!'

HAIL, HAIL, THE GANG'S ALL HALE!

The doctor returned from an hour-long laboratory examination of the oversize liquid specimen that Andrew McTavish had brought in that morning.

'You are a lucky man, McTavish,' the doctor said, 'there is not a bit of trouble in what you gave me to examine.'

'No albumen . . . no sugar?' asked the Scot.

'Nothing at all!' the doctor answered. 'You're as sound as a dollar!'

The Scot smiled happily. 'Would ye mind,' he asked, 'if I were to use yer phone to call up me wife?' The doctor gladly assented and soon McTavish had his wife on the wire.

'Och, Lassie! Good news! Neither you nor I nor Uncle Angus, nor Cousin Willie, nor even the boarder has a thing the matter wi' 'em!'

FINE POINT OF THE LAW

'It's too bad,' said the lawyer to the doctor, 'that, like some laws, birth control can't be retroactive.'

STOP THIEF!

Big Sam the patrolman on our block saw a man trotting down the street the other day with a leather couch on his back. 'A furniture thief!' said Big Sam and he ran after the man and soon caught up with him. He started to arrest him for possession of stolen goods.

'But I can prove this is my couch!' the man protested. 'I am a psychiatrist making a house call!'

DATING WITH A SHARP EYE

'A psychiatrist,' says Pamela Painless, the office nurse, 'is a chap who, when a pretty girl enters a room, watches everybody else!'

SMOOCH-O-PHOBIA

STUDENT NURSE: 'Don't kiss me . . . it's unsanitary!'

MEDICAL STUDENT: 'So what! I'm not doing this for my health!'

INJECTION OF MERRIMENT

Clancy was taking shots for his cold and every thing was going fine until he started adding beer chasers.

'I WILL *NOT* WET THE BED!
'I WILL *NOT* WET THE BED!
'I WILL *NOT* WET THE BED!'

'If you can't see *this*, you're blind!'

LECTURE NOTICE

The class of student nurses at Gettwel Hospital were studying pharmacy and the professor was giving them a lecture on the various plants that are used for medicinal extracts.

'Now you take this *"chinchona"* twig from which quinine is made,' the professor said and held up a small piece of wood. 'The twig you see here is made of bark, hardwood and pith. I'm sure you all know what pith is.'

The student nurses were silent.

'Come now,' the professor demanded, 'don't any of you would-be nurses know what pith is?' He turned to a girl in the front row.

'You there, Miss Sturdley, you know what pith is, don't you?'

'Yeth, thir!' said Miss Sturdley.

WHO'S ON THE MENU

She took the doctor's advice and almost had to take a rest cure. She thought he said that she needed three hearty *males* a day.

'Beg pardon, sailor, may I ask you for a little
assistance?'

'They *told* me you were a specialist!'

ONE LAST FLING

Twiddleham and Twickenham, two elderly play-boys, decided to have a final fling with two ladies of the chorus. As a kind of 'insurance policy' they visited a notorious quack doctor whose 'rejuvenator' tonic had been highly recommended by all the age-ing sports of their acquaintance.

'Take a dose of this before you go out on the town,' the charlatan doctor said, 'and you'll feel young enough for anything!'

The two old rips went back to their bachelor apartment and poured out a dose of the rejuvenator.

'Tell me, Twiddleham,' said the first playboy, 'are you beginning to feel any younger?'

'Dash my eyes, Twickenham,' answered his friend, 'I can't say that I do!'

'That doctor said that one dose would be enough,' Twickenham said, 'but I think we ought to try another.'

They both poured out another dose and sat back to await results. Nothing happened, so the two old sports took a third dose. After a moment Twicken-ham twitched and his face took on a curious expres-sion.

'Feeling younger?' his friend asked.

'Yes indeed,' he answered. 'In fact I've just done a very childish thing! Give me a moment to change my pants and we'll be off!'

'All right, dear patient, I will leave you. Now that your husband is home, I know you are in good hands!'

THE DOMINANT SEX

Ferris Splatt consulted Dr Froyd the psychiatrist one morning. He had a very unusual problem concerning his wife.

'Doctor,' he explained, 'my wife Brunhilde has suddenly developed an inferiority complex and, Doc, I've just got to find a way to keep her that way!'

NOT FIT FOR HUMAN CONSUMPTION

A navy base hospital received a radiogram from a ship at sea concerning a malnutrition case aboard.

ADVISE WHAT TO DO WITH CASE OF BERIBERI.

An apprentice signalman took it upon himself to wire back the following answer:

GIVE IT TO THE MASTER-AT-ARMS, HE'LL DRINK ANYTHING.

'. . . You say you have a seven-room flat for ten
pounds a month?'

HEALTHFUL HINT

If you can manage to drink a full glass of milk every day for 1,200 months and never miss once . . . you'll live to be a hundred!

WORDS TO AND FROM THE WISE

'The trouble with these medical school professors,' says Dr Spatula, 'is that too many of them have a diarrhoea of words along with a constipation of ideas.'

THE SAME GIRL

'Something wrong with your heart, young fellow,' the doctor said as he applied the stethoscope, 'you've had some trouble with Angina Pectoris, haven't you?'

'Yes, Doctor,' answered the young man, 'but that's not the way you pronounce her last name!'

'You'd better consult a psychiatrist, Madam!'

THE ONCE OVER TWICE

'Doc,' said the chorus girl, 'I thought I'd drop in for a thorough check-up. Can you tell me what my symptoms are, if any?'

The doctor smiled gently.

'Well now, Miss,' he said, 'you look pretty healthy to me but looking at you off-hand I'd say you have two things wrong with you: your slip is showing and you need glasses. That sign on my door says Veterinary Surgeon!'

NEEDS FIXIN'

They were worried about the ambulance at General Hospital. Seems that the engine was in poor shape. As the mechanic said to the head doctor one morning, 'Doc, our "meat wagon" is in a bad way! The carburettor won't carb, the spark plugs won't spark, the battery won't bat and the piston won't function either!'

A KNIFE TIME WAS HAD BY ALL

MEDICO: 'That man needs an operation badly!'

STUDENT NURSE: 'Don't you mean nicely, Doctor? The last man you operated on badly and he died!'

GOODY GOODY, A SAMARITAN!

Ellie Drizzle, student nurse, was very proud of her new-found knowledge even though she was only a first-year student. Passing along the street one day she saw a poorly dressed man lying face down over a pavement grating. Quickly the student nurse ran to him and began to administer artificial respiration. Almost immediately the man sat up.

'It worked!' she cried, 'I saved his life!'

'Saved my life nothing!' the man said indignantly. 'I was fishing for sixpences with chewing gum on a string!'

THE STRONG ARM OF THE LAW

Alphonse, of the celebrated French team of Alphonse and Gaston, found himself in London for the first time. Responding to a basic urge of nature Gaston looked around for one of those public conveniences that are a notable feature of Paris boulevards. But alas, after ten minutes of walking on tiptoe, he found none. In desperation Gaston slipped into a half-completed building only to find himself tapped on the shoulder by a policeman.

'No,' the bobby said, 'you can't do that 'ere Guv'nor!' and sent the Frenchman on his way.

A few minutes later a statue of the Duke of Wellington offered possibilities and just as Alphonse had slipped behind it another policeman stopped him and sent him away. An attempt behind a tree in Regent's Park was again frustrated by a policeman and poor Alphonse was about to give up hope when he saw a doctor's sign on a nearby house: J. Jones, MD, UROLOGIST.

Bounding up the stairs three at a time the frantic Frenchman burst into the consulting room crying out for help.

'Now what seems to be your trouble, my good man,' the MD asked.

'I cannot . . . how you say eet? . . . *relieve* myself, Docteur!' desperate Alphonse answered. Dr Jones handed Alphonse a glass container and requested him to step into the next room. Inside of a few seconds a hand reached out through the open door.

'Docteur!' came the voice of Alphonse, 'another containaire, please!' The doctor handed in what was requested, and a few moments later came another request for a 'containaire', and so on until the astonished doctor had handed in five containers.

'Well, sir!' the doctor said as the now smiling Alphonse came out of the room, 'who told you that you could not relieve yourself?'

'Ze whole Metropolitan Police Force!'

PHYSICIAN'S PHYSICAL

The army doctor was examining a candidate for the WRAC. As he filled in the routine report, he fired the usual questions at the pretty candidate.

Name:
Jones
First Name:
Jane
Date and place of birth:
June 21st, 1935, Brighton.
Eyes?
Blue
Hair?
Red
Sex?

At this question she hesitated, then blushing said 'Infrequently'.

LIFE ON THE BOUNCING WAVE

A pair of Siamese twins came into Dr Killkare's office for an examination. The twins, both of middle age, had shiny bald heads and they asked the doctor to treat some very bad lumps and bruises that were disfiguring their shiny skulls.

The doctor gave the necessary treatment then said, 'Tell me, gentlemen, how did this happen?'

The twins smiled at one another then the right one answered: 'You won't believe this, Doctor, but this is the way it happened! My twin brother and I were fishing in Wampum Lake when our rowboat overturned. We started to go under and a speedboat came dashing to our rescue. Trouble was, every time my brother and I poked our hairless heads above the surface of the water the jerk in the motorboat would beat us with an oar and yell: 'Go under again, you indecent pig, and come up the RIGHT way! Don't you see there's ladies present?'

SCATTERBRAIN

The young widow was terribly embarrassed over the phone. 'Doctor,' she said in a hesitant voice, 'you remember I was at your office this morning for a thorough physical examination? Well, did you by any chance find a pair of . . . pink nylon panties . . ? No? You're *sure*, Doctor? Oh, my goodness, I must have left them at the dentist's!'

'You tell your teacher that she's got a dilated pupil!'

AFTER YOU

Madame Haricot Vert came to consult the leading baby doctor of Paris with a special problem concerning her unborn child. 'Docteur,' she explained, 'my husband Pierre is a good man and a rich man but he has one terrible fault, he is very impolite and given to bad language. I am afraid that my little child will grow up to be a rude and coarse man like his father. How can I prevent this?'

The doctor thought for a while then made the following suggestion. 'Madame, you know about pre-natal suggestion which is when you do something every day to suggest to the unborn child some good influence, therefore I think you should point to your stomach every hour on the hour and say: "Be POLITE!" This will influence the baby, I am sure!'

Madame Haricot Vert went home and from then on she never missed an hour, and pointed faithfully to her unborn child saying over and over again: 'Be POLITE!'

Soon her term came but no birth resulted. She soon went a month past her term. No child. After three months and no baby she was a medical curiosity. After a year and no baby she was famous. Two years went by and the ever-pregnant Madame Haricot Vert continued to astonish the medical world. She was in good health and the child was still alive inside her. After five years, the academy of medicine decided to operate on her and discover why the child did not appear. Accordingly a full-dress operation was staged with all the chief doctors of France to witness it. There the doctors found two healthy twin boys bowing to each other with elaborate politeness and saying: 'After you, my dear Gaston!' – 'Non! It is after YOU, my dear Alphonse!'

I DON'T WANT TO GET WELL . . .

Young Wolfish was due for an operation, and while he was waiting for the big day he found himself being taken care of by a very beautiful young nurse.

'Nurse,' said Wolfish, on the morning before his operation, 'I'm really crazy for you . . . I don't care if I never get well!'

'Maybe you won't,' answered the nurse. 'The doctor who is going to operate on you is my fiancé, and he saw you kissing me this morning!'

SAME OLD STORY

DENTIST: 'Sorry, honey, but I'm all out of gas!'
GIRLIE: 'Oh, not *you* too!'

MUSIC HATH CHARMS

The man forced his way into the doctor's surgery without waiting his turn.

'Doctor, you must help me!' he gasped. Seeing how distraught the man was the doctor decided to humour him, and asked him what his trouble was.

'Well you see,' the man blurted out, 'I have a very embarrassing condition . . . every time I kiss my wife I have an uncontrollable urge to shout WOW!'

The doctor nodded sympathetically then asked the man if he wouldn't wait in the next room until he had seen all of the remaining patients. When the man had gone the doctor resumed his examinations and soon forgot about his excited visitor. At that point a woman rushed in in great excitement and interrupted the doctor with a tale of woe. The doctor, seeing how upset she was listened sympathetically.

'My problem, Doctor,' she said in a tearful voice, 'is that when I fulfil the role of a wife I have a terrible compulsion to sing out loud:

HOLD THAT TIGER!
HOLD THAT TIGER!

And, Doctor, this may break up my marriage!'

The MD explained that hers was a complicated emotional problem that would require his careful thought, and would she be kind enough to step into the next room and wait until he had finished with the remaining patients. The woman agreed, and the doctor resumed his work.

The last patient finally left and the doctor leaned

Kyle Onstott
MANDINGO   30P
DRUM   35P
MASTER OF FALCONHURST   35P
Kyle Onstott & Lance Horner
FALCONHURST FANCY   35P
Lance Horner
HEIR TO FALCONHURST   40P

ROMANTIC FICTION
Jean Plaidy
MADAME SERPENT   30P
THE WANDERING PRINCE   30P
GAY LORD ROBERT   30P
MURDER MOST ROYAL   35P
Georgette Heyer
COUSIN KATE   30P
FREDERICA   30P
BATH TANGLE   30P
Sergeanne Golon
THE TEMPTATION OF ANGELIQUE: Book One
The Jesuit Trap   30P
THE TEMPTATION OF ANGELIQUE: Book Two
Gold Beard's Downfall   30P
THE COUNTESS ANGELIQUE: Book One
In The Land Of The Redskins   30P
THE COUNTESS ANGELIQUE: Book Two
Prisoner Of The Mountains   30P

HISTORICAL FICTION
Frederick E. Smith
WATERLOO   25P
Jack Olsen
SILENCE ON MONTE SOLE   35P

NON-FICTION

Dr. Laurence J. Peter & Raymond Hull
THE PETER PRINCIPLE   30p
Peter F. Drucker
THE AGE OF DISCONTINUITY   60p
Jim Dante & Leo Diegel
THE NINE BAD SHOTS OF GOLF (illus.)   35p
Dr. A. Ward Gardner & Dr. Peter J. Roylance
NEW SAFETY AND FIRST-AID (illus.)   30p
William Sargant
THE UNQUIET MIND   45p
Paul Davies
THE FIELD AT WATERLOO (illus.)   25p
Graham Hill
LIFE AT THE LIMIT (illus.)   35p
Ken Welsh
HITCH-HIKER'S GUIDE TO EUROPE (illus.)   35p
Miss Read
MISS READ'S COUNTRY COOKING (illus.)   30p
Gavin Maxwell
RAVEN SEEK THY BROTHER (illus.)   30p

Obtainable from all booksellers and newsagents. If you
have any difficulty, please send purchase price plus 5p
postage to P.O. Box 11, Falmouth, Cornwall. While
every effort is made to keep prices low, it is sometimes
necessary to increase prices at short notice. PAN Books
reserve the right to show new retail prices on covers
which may differ from the text or elsewhere.

I enclose a cheque/postal order for selected titles ticked
above plus 5p to cover postage and packing.

NAME ....

ADDRESS ....